# Science Fair Projects About Planet Earth

**Robert Gardner**

**Enslow Publishing**
101 W. 23rd Street
Suite 240
New York, NY 10011
USA
enslow.com

Published in 2017 by Enslow Publishing, LLC.
101 W. 23rd Street, Suite 240, New York, NY 10011

**Library of Congress Cataloging-in-Publication Data**

Names: Gardner, Robert, 1929– author.
Title: Science fair projects about planet Earth / Robert Gardner.
Description: New York, NY : Enslow Publishing, 2017. | Series: Hands-on science | Audience: Ages 8+. | Audience: Grades 4 to 6. | Includes bibliographical references and index.
Identifiers: LCCN 2016019993 | ISBN 9780766082199 (library bound) | ISBN 9780766082243 (pbk.) | ISBN 9780766082250 (6-pack)
Subjects: LCSH: Earth science projects—Juvenile literature. | Earth sciences—Experiments—Juvenile literature. | Science projects—Juvenile literature.
Classification: LCC QE29 .G377 2017 | DDC 550.78—dc23
LC record available at https://lccn.loc.gov/2016019993

Printed in China

**To Our Readers:** We have done our best to make sure all website addresses in this book were active and appropriate when we went to press. However, the author and the publisher have no control over and assume no liability for the material available on those websites or on any websites they may link to. Any comments or suggestions can be sent by e-mail to customerservice@enslow.com.

Portions of this book originally appeared in the book *Earth-Shaking Science Projects About Planet Earth*.

**Photo Credits:** Cover, p. 1 Denis Tabler/Shutterstock.com (Earth on blue); Dr_Flash/Shutterstock.com (Earth on black on back cover); Strejman/Shutterstock.com (handprint on spine); design elements throughout book: ctrlaplus/Shutterstock.com (quote bubbles), Bimbim/Shutterstock.com (science doodles in blue background), Sergey Nivens/Shutterstock.com (lightbulb), Paul Velgos/Shutterstock.com (notebook), StepanPopov/Shutterstock.com (question marks); p. 4 Aphelleon/Shutterstock.com.

**Illustrations by Joseph Hill.**

# Contents

# Introduction

**E**arth seems to be flat. Just look! But we know it is round. How did we discover that it is round?

Inside Earth are layers of rocks, liquids, and metals. Why are there layers?

We live on one of several huge, rocky plates that are slowly moving. We do not feel that motion, but if we lived for millions of years, we would see that whole continents move. What makes these huge plates move? How do they cause earthquakes and volcanoes? How do they make mountains? By doing the experiments in this book, you will find the answers to these questions, and you will learn much, much more.

## Entering a Science Fair

Some experiments in this book have ideas for science fair projects. However, judges at science fairs like experiments that are creative, so do not simply copy an experiment in this book. Expand on one of the ideas suggested, or develop a project of your own. Choose something you really like and want to know more about. It will be more interesting to you, and it can lead to a creative experiment that you plan and carry out.

Before entering a science fair, read one or more of the books listed under Further Reading. They will give you helpful hints and lots of useful information about science fairs.

## Safety First

*To do experiments safely always follow these rules:*

**1** Always do experiments **under adult supervision**.

**2** Read all instructions carefully. If you have questions, **check with the adult**.

**3** Be serious when experimenting. Fooling around can be dangerous to you and to others.

**4** Keep the area where you work clean and organized. When you have finished, clean up and put all of your materials away.

# The Shape of Planet Earth

## Things You Will Need:

- ocean or one of the Great Lakes
- view of ship sailing away from shore
- scissors
- Styrofoam cup
- toothpick
- large, round ball, such as a soccer ball or basketball
- a friend
- a flat table

*How do we know that Earth is round? Write down your answers and your reasons for them.*

## Let's Investigate!

**1** Do you live near the ocean or one of the Great Lakes? If you do, watch a tall ship as it sails away from shore. Which part of the ship disappears first? Which part disappears last? Would what you see happen if Earth were flat instead of round?

**2** If you cannot watch a tall ship sail to the horizon, try this. It is what you would see if you could watch ships sail to the horizon. Using scissors, cut a small piece from the rim of a Styrofoam cup.

**3** Stick a toothpick in the Styrofoam. The toothpick represents the mast or stack of a ship.

**4** Put your eye level with the top of a large ball. Have a friend slowly move the "ship" over the top of the ball. What happened as the ship moved beyond the top of the ball?

**5** Repeat the experiment on a flat table. What is different?

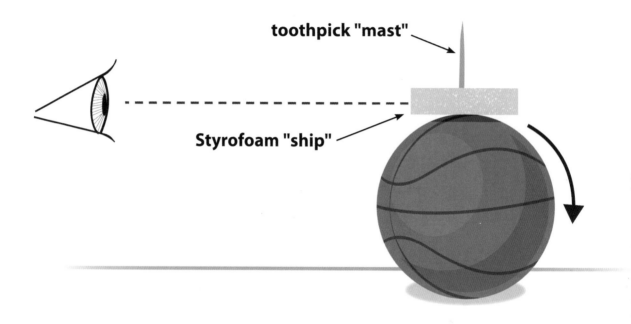

toothpick "mast"

Styrofoam "ship"

# The Shape of Planet Earth: The Facts

Today we have pictures of Earth taken from space, but people knew Earth was round long before astronauts flew into space. They could see the bottom of a ship disappear below the horizon before the mast. Also, stars not seen before would appear above the horizon as they sailed north or south. Only a round Earth could explain these sights. On a flat Earth, objects would simply grow smaller with distance. Their lower parts would not disappear before their upper parts. And, on a flat Earth, the same stars would be seen everywhere.

**This star cannot be seen until the ship reaches point 3.**

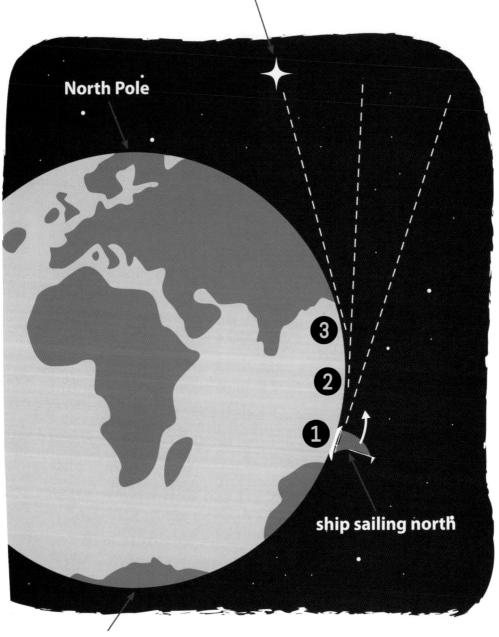

North Pole

3

2

1

ship sailing north

South Pole

# More Evidence of a Round Earth

## Things You Will Need:

- a dark room
- lightbulb
- light-colored wall
- sphere, such as a large ball
- Frisbee or jar lid
- a cylinder, such as a tin can
- a cone, such as an empty ice cream cone

*Aristotle (384–322 BCE), an early Greek scientist, believed that Earth was a sphere (shaped like a ball). During an eclipse of the moon (when Earth lines up between the sun and the moon), Earth's shadow moves across the moon. Aristotle saw that the shadow's edge was always curved like the edge of a circle. He said that only a sphere always casts a round shadow.*

*Do you think that a sphere always casts a round shadow? Write down your ideas and your reasons for them.*

## Let's Investigate!

**1** Go to a dark room. Turn on a single lightbulb near one side of the room. The light will cast shadows of objects held near a wall on the other side of the room.

**2** Hold a sphere, such as a soccer or beach ball, near the wall. Turn it in different ways. Does the sphere *always* cast a round shadow?

**3** Make shadows using other objects with round sides. You might use a Frisbee, a jar lid, a cylinder, and a cone. Can these objects cast round shadows? Can they cast shadows with other shapes? If so, how many different shadow shapes can they make? Do any of these objects *always* cast a round shadow?

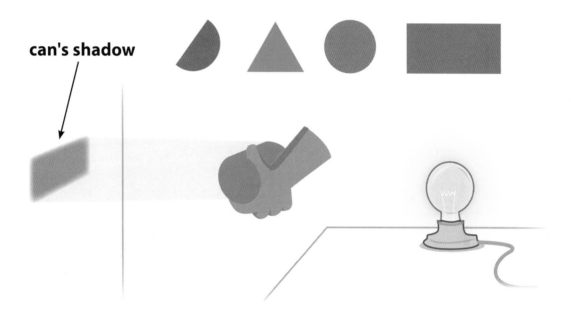

**can's shadow**

# More Evidence of a Round Earth: The Facts

In your experiment, only a sphere *always* casts a round shadow. A disk, such as a Frisbee or a lid, can cast shadows with other shapes. The same is true of cylinders and cones. You can easily cast rectangular shadows with a cylinder and triangular shadows with a cone. Aristotle was right! Only a sphere always casts a round shadow.

S
U
N
L
I
G
H
T

During an eclipse of the moon, Earth's round shadow falls on the moon.

## Idea for Your Science Fair

- Design models and carry out experiments to show that Earth is round.

# 3

# Let's Look Inside Earth

**Things You Will Need:**

- an adult
- hard-boiled egg
- sharp, wet knife
- broad-tipped marking pen

*What do you think is between you and Earth's center? Write down your ideas and your reasons for them.*

**Let's Investigate!**

1. Use a hard-boiled egg as a model. Gently tap the egg against something hard until cracks appear in the shell. The shell represents Earth's rocky outer layer, its crust. The cracks you see represent the edges of the rocky plates that make up Earth's crust.

2. **Ask an adult** to use a sharp, wet knife to cut the egg in half. The white part of the egg represents what is below Earth's crust. It is called the mantle and is made up of rocks. Although rocks are normally hard, rocks in the mantle can become liquid when very hot.

3. Using a broad-tipped marking pen, make a solid circle in the center of the yolk as shown in the drawing. The circle represents Earth's inner core. The rest of the yolk represents Earth's outer core. The core is believed to be mostly iron and some nickel. The outer core is liquid metal. The inner core is mostly solid and very hot. Temperatures there are nearly as hot as the surface of the sun, which is a hundred times hotter than a hot summer day on Earth.

4. Compare your egg model with the cutaway Earth diagram. How is it similar? Different? What do its parts show?

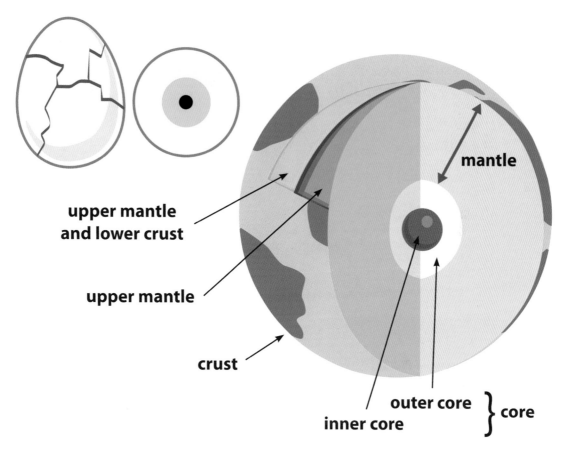

upper mantle
and lower crust

mantle

upper mantle

crust

outer core } core

inner core

# Let's Look Inside Earth: **The Facts**

Six large plates and more than a dozen small plates cover Earth's surface and the oceans' bottoms. They are made up of the rocky crust and the upper part of Earth's mantle. Rocks in the mantle are heavier than those in the crust. The plates, which "float" on the mantle, move slowly (an inch or less per year). The outer core contains melted metals that move. Scientists know very little about the inner core, but it is believed to be mostly solid iron and nickel.

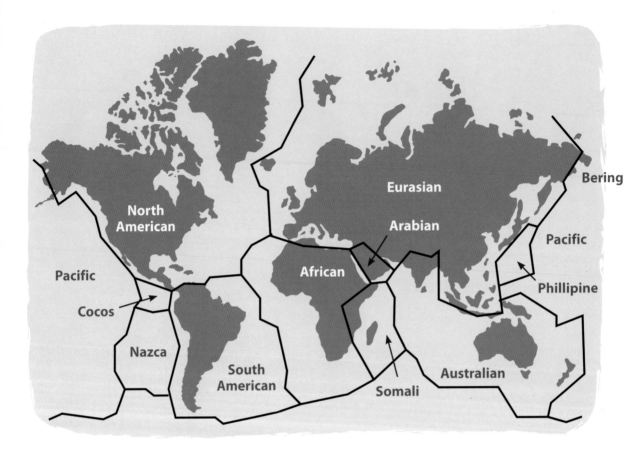

This map shows the names and locations of Earth's plates.

## Idea for Your Science Fair

- Can you build a three-dimensional scale mode that represents Earth from its surface to its center?

# 4

# How Do Earth's Layers Differ?

## Things You Will Need:

- cold water
- short, wide, 6- or 8-ounce drinking glass
- measuring cup
- measuring tablespoon
- spoon for stirring
- kosher salt
- green food coloring
- baster
- cooking oil
- thumbtacks

*What is different about Earth's layers? Write down your ideas and your reasons for them.*

**Let's Investigate!**

1. Pour 1/2 cup of cold water into a short, wide, 6- or 8-ounce drinking glass.

2. Pour 1/2 cup of water into a measuring cup. Add 2 tablespoons of kosher salt. Stir with a spoon until the salt dissolves (disappears). Add 4 drops of green food coloring and stir.

3. Remove some of the green salt water using a baster. Carefully place the tip of the baster on the bottom of the water in the drinking glass. Very slowly, squeeze the bulb of the baster. This will put the green liquid under the clear water. Be careful not to release your squeeze on the bulb as you take the baster out of the water. Look at the glass from the side. How many layers do you have?

4. Carefully put 2 tablespoons of cooking oil on the clear water. How many layers do you have now?

5. Drop some thumbtacks into the drinking glass. What happens to the tacks? How many layers do you have now?

What layers of Earth are represented by the layers in the glass? After doing this experiment, what do you think is different about Earth's layers?

salt water

cold water

# How Do Earth's Layers Differ?
## *The Facts*

The table below shows how the layers you made represent Earth's layers.

| Layer in Glass | Earth Layer Represented |
| --- | --- |
| Cooking oil | Crust |
| Clear water | Mantle |
| Green salt water | Outer core |
| Thumbtacks | Inner core |

Thumbtacks sink in cooking oil, water, and salt water. In the same way, the metals in Earth's inner core sink in Earth's outer core, mantle, and crust. Just as cooking oil floats on water and salt water, so Earth's crust floats on its mantle.

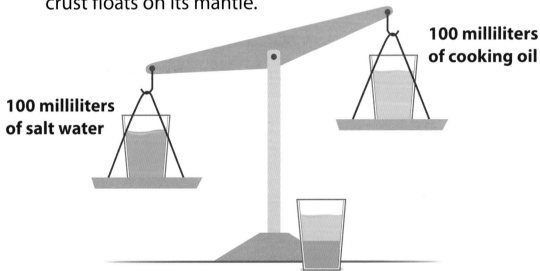

100 milliliters of cooking oil

100 milliliters of salt water

How does the drawing of the balance help explain why oil floats on water?

# 5

# Continents on the Move

**Things You Will Need:**

- map of the world
- tracing paper
- pencil
- scissors
- construction paper

*South America and Africa are continents. Look at them on a world map. Do you think they might once have been joined? Why or why not? Write down your ideas and your reasons for them.*

1 Find a good map of the world. Place a sheet of tracing paper on South America. Use a sharp pencil to trace this continent. Do the same for Africa.

2 Use scissors to cut out the shapes of both continents. Then use the cutouts to cut the shapes of the two continents from construction paper. How well do the two continents fit together?

3 Using the same method, cut out the shapes of the other continents—North America, Australia, Antarctica, and Eurasia. Think of Europe and Asia as one continent.

4 View the continents as pieces of a puzzle. How well do they fit together?

Do you think all the continents might once have been joined? (The fits may not be perfect. Ocean levels and the edges of continents have changed with time.) Which continents do you think were the last to separate from one another? What makes you think so? Save Africa and South America for the next experiment.

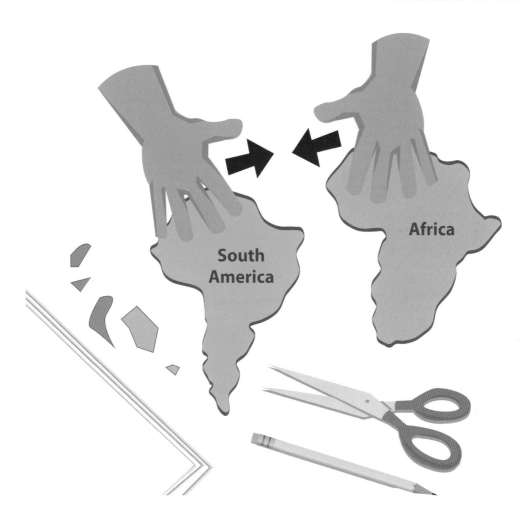

## Continents on the Move:
## The Facts

Geologists and biologists think that there was just one continent 250 million years ago. They call it Pangaea. Since then, Pangaea has separated into the continents we know today. Oceans or narrow strips of land lie between continents that were once joined together.

You probably found that Africa and South America fit together best. It is reasonable to think that these two continents were the last to separate. Ocean levels and erosion would have had less time to cause changes in their shapes.

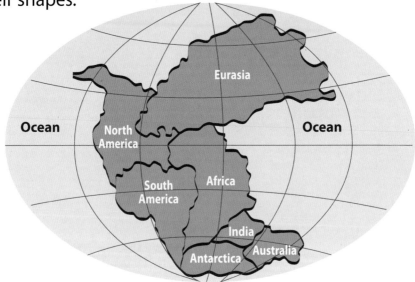

**Pangaea (250 million years ago) with Earth's plates joined**

# Ideas for Your Science Fair

- **What evidence do geologists have that all the continents were once joined?**

- **What evidence do biologists have that all the continents were once joined?**

# 6

# What Makes Continents Move?

## Things You Will Need:

- construction paper
- cutouts from Experiment 5
- clay
- short, wide glass
- cold water
- hot water
- measuring cup marked in ounces
- green food coloring
- dropper

*What do you think makes continents move? Write down your ideas and your reasons for them.*

# Let's Investigate!

**1** Make 4 or 5 pleated (fan-like) folds in a sheet of construction paper (see drawing). Place the cutouts of Africa and South America from Experiment 5 on the folded pleats. The continents should be touching as they were in Pangaea. Add small lumps of clay to give the continents some weight. The folded paper represents Earth's mantle, although the mantle is not really folded.

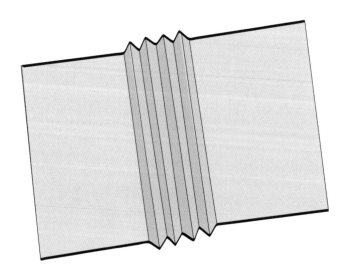

**2** Slowly pull the ends of the paper apart. What happens to the continents? What does the new space between the continents represent?

**3** To see why geologists think the continents move, try this: Nearly fill a short, wide glass with cold water. Put about 1 ounce of hot water into a measuring cup. Add green food coloring until the hot water is quite dark.

**4** Fill a dropper with the hot, green water. Slowly squeeze the hot, green water underneath the cold water. Keep squeezing on the dropper bulb as you remove it from the cold water. Watch the hot water. It represents hot matter inside Earth's mantle. What happens to it? How could what you see explain the movement of continents?

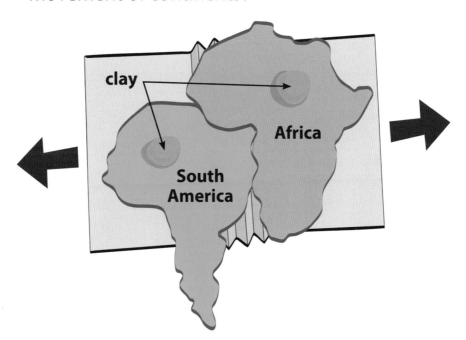

# What Makes Continents Move?
## *The Facts*

Continents make up part of Earth's crust. The crust is divided into plates. The plates float on the mantle. Rocks in the mantle may become so hot they change to a liquid. The rocks expand (get bigger) when they become a liquid. This makes them rise and spread out under Earth's crust. This movement of hot matter is called convection. The liquid rocks move like the hot water you put under cold water. The hot liquid in the mantle may push Earth's plates apart, making them move very slowly. Any continent on a plate will move, too.

**Green hot water rises in cold water and spreads out. Hot magma can move in the same way.**

# 7

# When Earth's Plates Separate

## Things You Will Need:

- 1-gallon clear, resealable plastic bag
- table or counter
- 2 heavy books
- a partner

*Suppose two of Earth's plates began to move apart. What do you think might happen? Write down your ideas and your reasons for them.*

1 Find a 1-gallon clear plastic bag that can be sealed. Allow a small amount of air to enter the bag. Then seal the bag so the air cannot get out.

2 Put the bag on a table or counter. Place 2 heavy books on the bag. The book bindings should touch. The books represent two of Earth's plates that meet. The air in the bag represents magma (hot melted rocks from the mantle).

3 Put your eye level with the table or counter. Have a partner slowly pull the books apart as shown in the drawing. What happens to the "magma" (air) between the "plates" (books)? After doing this experiment, what do you think might happen when two of Earth's plates separate?

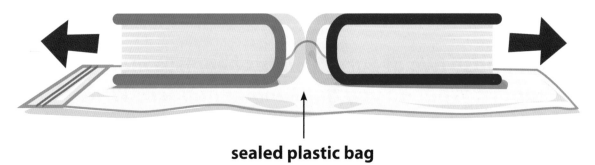

**sealed plastic bag**

# When Earth's Plates Separate: The Facts

As the books were pulled apart, air, representing magma, came up between them. When two plates separate, there is a weakness in Earth's crust. Hot magma from Earth's mantle may come up between the plates. As the liquid magma cools, it adds new crust to the plates. It can also form mountains. For example, the Mid-Atlantic Ridge is a line of mountains under the Atlantic Ocean. It marks the boundary between the African and South American plates. There are other mountains under the seas. These mountains often mark the cracks in Earth's crust—the places where Earth's plates meet.

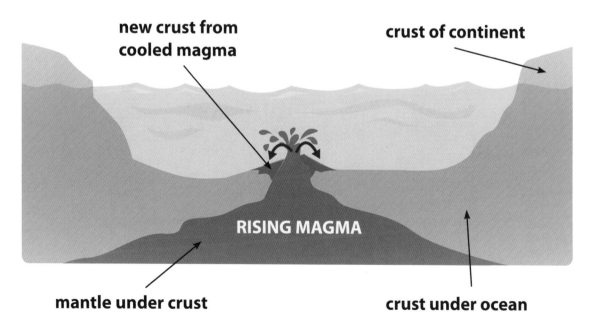

new crust from cooled magma

crust of continent

RISING MAGMA

mantle under crust

crust under ocean

# 8

# More Plate Movements

## Things You Will Need:

- thin book with shiny cover
- thick book with shiny cover
- smooth counter
- 4 graham crackers
- drinking glass
- water
- wax paper

*You have seen what happens when plates move apart. In what other ways do you think plates might move? Write down your ideas and your reasons for them.*

## Let's Investigate!

**1** Find a thin book and a thick book. Both should have shiny covers. Put their spines together on a smooth counter. The books represent two of Earth's plates. Push the two books toward each other. What happens? What might happen when two of Earth's plates get pushed together?

**2** Dip the ends of two graham crackers in a glass of water. Put the two wet ends side by side on wax paper on a smooth counter. Slowly push the crackers together. What happens? What do the crackers represent? What else might happen when two of Earth's plates get pushed together?

**3** Put two more graham crackers side by side on a smooth counter. The crackers represent two of Earth's plates. Hold the plates firmly together. Then try to slide them past each other as shown in the drawing. What happens? How else might two of Earth's plates move when they are side by side?

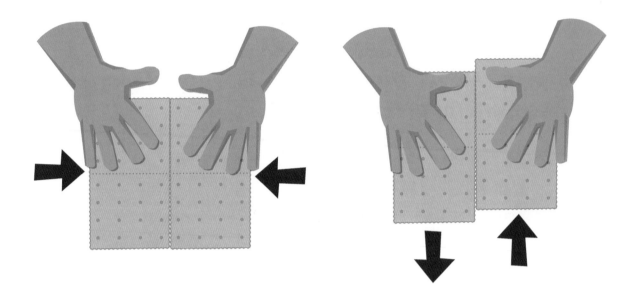

# More Plate Movements: *The Facts*

Earth's plates can be pushed together, and they can slide past one another. If they are pushed together, the lighter plate may slide under the heavier one. You saw this happen when you pushed the two books together.

Two plates can come together pushing up rocks and soil to form mountains. This can cause earthquakes. You saw this happen when you pushed the two wet crackers together.

When you made the crackers slide past each other, they tended to stick together. When you pushed harder, they suddenly slipped by one another. When Earth's plates do this, they create vibrations that shake Earth's surface. We call these vibrations earthquakes.

Colliding plates can slowly make mountains or earthquakes.

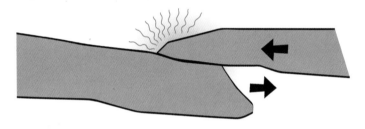

One plate sliding under another can make lots of heat.

Plates slipping past each other can cause earthquakes.

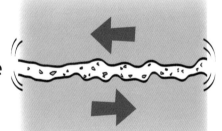

## Idea for Your Science Fair

● Find other ways to show how Earth's plates move and what effects the movements can have.

# 9

# Effects of an Earthquake

- lid from a large shoebox
- pencil or pen
- books that can be stacked
- sugar cubes

*Moving plates can shake Earth's crust. How can you make a model to show the effects of an earthquake? Write down your ideas and your reasons for them.*

## Let's Investigate!

**1** Find the lid of a large shoebox. The lid represents part of Earth's crust.

**2** Make a mark at the center of the inside of the lid. The point represents an epicenter. An epicenter is a point on Earth's surface. It is directly above the place where an earthquake occurs.

**3** Place the ends of the lid on stacks of books that are the same height.

**4** Use sugar cubes to make "buildings." The buildings can be two, three, and four stories tall. Place all the buildings on the lid at the same distance from the epicenter.

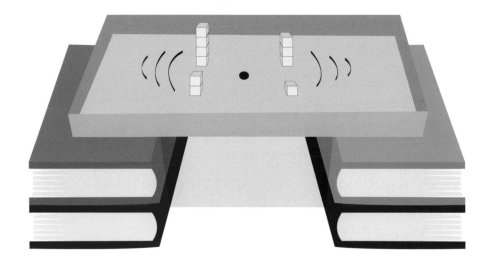

**5** Using your finger, tap the underside of the lid at the epicenter. Your tapping represents an earthquake. Which sugar cube building falls first? Which is the last?

**6** Repeat the experiment. Are your results the same?

**7** Now do another experiment. Make only two-story buildings, but put them at different distances from the epicenter. Now tap again.

Are the results the same? Why or why not?

What can you do to make more buildings survive an earthquake?

# Effects of an Earthquake: The Facts

When Earth's crust moves suddenly, it makes vibrations. The vibrations move through the crust like waves. The waves weaken as they move away from the epicenter. It's like when you throw a stone into a pond.

When "buildings" of different heights are the same distance from the epicenter, the tallest ones often fall first. Was this true in your experiment?

To see how distance affects the strength of an earthquake, you put "buildings" of the same height at different distances from the epicenter. You did that because a good experiment tests only one thing at a time. Perhaps you found that the buildings closest to the epicenter fell first.

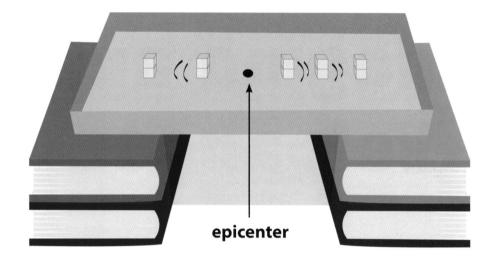

epicenter

# Ideas for Your Science Fair

- Find out how buildings are designed to resist earthquakes.

- Build models to show how buildings can be made to resist earthquakes.

- What is a tsunami? What causes it? What were the effects of the tsunami that struck Japan on March 11, 2011?

# 10

# Magma and Volcanoes

## Things You Will Need:

- empty plastic vitamin bottle, 8–10 ounce size
- clay (optional)
- a sink
- measuring tablespoon
- baking soda
- red food coloring
- measuring cup
- vinegar

*Heat is produced inside Earth and by moving plates. This heat melts rocks in Earth's mantle. The melted rocks (magma) expand (take up more space). The hot magma may push up through weak places in Earth's crust, creating a volcano. How can you make a model to represent a volcano? Write down your ideas and your reasons for them.*

## Let's Investigate!

**1** Find an empty plastic vitamin bottle. If you want, you can make the bottle look more like a volcano. Use clay to form a cone around the bottle.

**2** Put the soon-to-be volcano in a sink. Pour a tablespoonful of baking soda into the bottle. Add 10 drops of red food coloring.

**3** Pour one-quarter cup of vinegar into the bottle. Watch and listen! What happens?

**4** Feel the side of the bottle. What do you feel?

**5** How is your model like a real volcano? How is it not like a real volcano?

**6** Rinse the bottle with running water and discard.

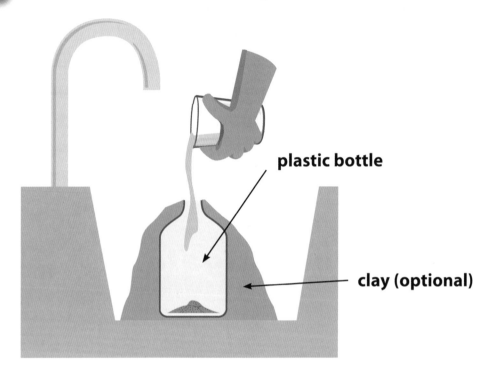

plastic bottle

clay (optional)

# Magma and Volcanoes: *The Facts*

The hot magma that flows up through Earth's crust is called lava after it reaches Earth's surface. In your experiment, you heard sounds as a reddish liquid with bubbles of gas erupted from the "volcano." When you felt the bottle, you probably found that it was cool. A real volcano also makes noise as red-hot magma mixed with gases erupts from its vent (opening). However, a real volcano is much bigger, hotter, and more violent. Also, the liquid lava, which isn't fizzy bubbles of gas, slowly cools and becomes solid rocks.

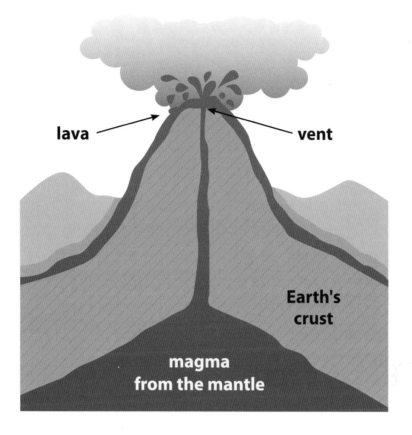

lava — vent

Earth's crust

magma from the mantle

# Ideas for Your Science Fair

- Find other ways to make a model volcano.

- A volcano can change Earth's surface by creating a mountain of lava rocks. How do glaciers change Earth's surface?

# Glossary

**convection**  The movement of a liquid or gas caused by heating.

**earthquake**  A shaking of Earth's crust caused by the movement of Earth's plates.

**eclipse**  A darkening of the moon when Earth's shadow falls on it. Or a darkening of the sun when the moon's shadow falls on Earth.

**epicenter**  A point on Earth's surface that is directly above the place where an earthquake occurs.

**fault**  A break in Earth's crust.

**inner core**  The innermost part of Earth that is mostly very hot, solid metals (iron and nickel).

**lava**  Magma that has flowed onto Earth's surface.

**magma**  Hot liquid rocks beneath Earth's surface.

**outer core**  A layer of liquid metal, mostly iron and some nickel, that lies below the mantle.

**Pangaea**  A continent that existed long ago when all the present continents were joined.

**plates**  Parts of Earth's crust that can move.

**vent**  An opening in a volcano through which magma flows to Earth's surface.

**volcano**  An opening in Earth's crust that allows magma to reach Earth's surface.

# Further Reading

## Books

Ardley, Neil. *101 Great Science Experiments.* New York, NY: DK Ltd., 2014.

Buczynski, Sandy. *Designing a Winning Science Fair Project.* Ann Arbor, MI: Cherry Lake Publishing, 2014.

Dickmann, Nancy. *Exploring Planet Earth and the Moon.* New York, NY: Rosen Publishing's Rosen Central, 2016.

Hyde, Natalie. *Earthquakes, Eruptions, and Other Events that Change Earth.* New York, NY: Crabtree Publishing Co., 2016.

Katirgis, Jane. *Eerie Earthquakes.* New York, NY: Enslow Publishing, Inc., 2016.

Latta, Sara. *All About Earth: Exploring the Planet with Science Projects.* North Mankato, MN: Capstone Press, 2016.

McGill, Jordan. *Earth Science Fair Projects.* New York, NY: AV2 by Weigl, 2012.

Sohn, Emily. *Experiments in Earth Science and Weather.* North Mankato, MN: Capstone Press, 2016.

## Websites

**A2Z Homeschooling.**
homeschooling.gomilpitas.com/directory/EarthScience.htm
*A directory of earth science experiments on topics including the atmosphere, biomes, and geology.*

**Kids.gov**
kids.usa.gov/science/our-planet/index.shtml
*Read facts, watch videos, play games, and do projects about Earth and its environment.*

**NASA**
climatekids.nasa.gov
*NASA's Climate Kids: NASA's Eyes on the Earth is filled with links and games about air, weather, water, energy, plants, and animals.*

# Index

## A
Africa, 24–26, 28, 33
Antarctica, 24, 26
Aristotle, 12–13
Atlantic Ocean, 33
Australia, 24, 26

## C
continents
    movement of,
        27–30
    shape of, 23–26
convection, 30
crust, 16–17, 22, 30,
    33, 38–40, 43–44

## E
Earth
    inside, 15–18
    shape of, 7–14
earthquakes, 5, 36–37
    effects of, 38–41
eclipse, 12, 14
epicenter, 39–41
Eurasia, 24, 26

## G
glaciers, 45

## I
inner core, 16–17, 22
iron, 16–17

## L
lava, 44–45

layers, differences
    between, 19–22

## M
magma, 30, 32–33,
    42–45
mantle, 16–17, 22,
    28–30, 32–33, 43,
    45
Mid-Atlantic Ridge, 33
moon, the, 12, 14
mountains, 5, 33,
    36–37, 45

## N
nickel, 16–17
North America, 24, 26

## O
outer core, 16–17, 22

## P
Pangaea, 25–26, 28
plates, 5, 16–18, 26, 30,
    38, 43
    movement of,
        34–37
    separation of, 31–33

## S
safety rules, 6
science fair projects,
    5–6, 14, 18, 26, 37,
    41, 45
shadows, 12–14

South America, 23–26,
    28–29, 33
stars, 9
sun, the, 12, 16

## T
tsunami, 41

## V
volcanoes, 5, 42–45